THE TRIPLETS
GO TO SCHOOL

Mercé Company • *Roser Capdevila*

GIVE US BOOKS
GIVE US WINGS
1989 YEAR OF THE YOUNG READER

DERRYDALE BOOKS
New York

To start with, Mommy took us to a store to buy our cotton school smocks. They had them in many different colors. The saleslady said that we were very bright and charming. We were very, very good.

4

They called our classroom the Nursery Room. It was very sunny with little, low tables. Can you see us? I always take my doll with me. Anna never goes anywhere without her little blanket, and Ellen always has her pacifier.

5

We didn't like sitting still all the time so they let us go out into the playground. It was much bigger than where we play at home. And it had a slide and a swing. I showed everyone how to slither down the slide. Anna found a water faucet and figured out how to turn it on. We had so much fun!

Later on, we went to the washroom. Ellen was crying because she'd fallen off the swing and had a scratch on her bottom but our teacher soon fixed it up. The sinks and the toilets were low, low down, made especially for little children like us.

9

Soon it was lunchtime.
We were so hungry that our stomachs were grumbling.
This was our very first meal at school.
And it certainly was full of surprises!

After such an exciting lunch we got very sleepy and the teacher made us all lie down on little cots. It was all so much fun that we weren't tired anymore, so instead of sleeping, we began to play.

14

The day flew by. When it was time to go home our teacher helped us put on our jackets, hung our bags over our shoulders, and told us not to move until Mommy came to get us. But we soon got tired of waiting and decided to walk home by ourselves.

Of course, we got lost, but a nice policeman found us and took us to the police station. He and his partners gave us some candies and let us eat as many as we wanted. They tried to make us laugh, but all three of us were very tired and we started to cry for our Mommy and Daddy. When they finally came we were very, very happy to see them.

After we'd been going to school for a few days we all got sick. The doctor said we had the measles. We laughed at each other when we saw all those little red spots and we even painted a few more on ourselves with a colored pencil. Being sick together was fun, too!

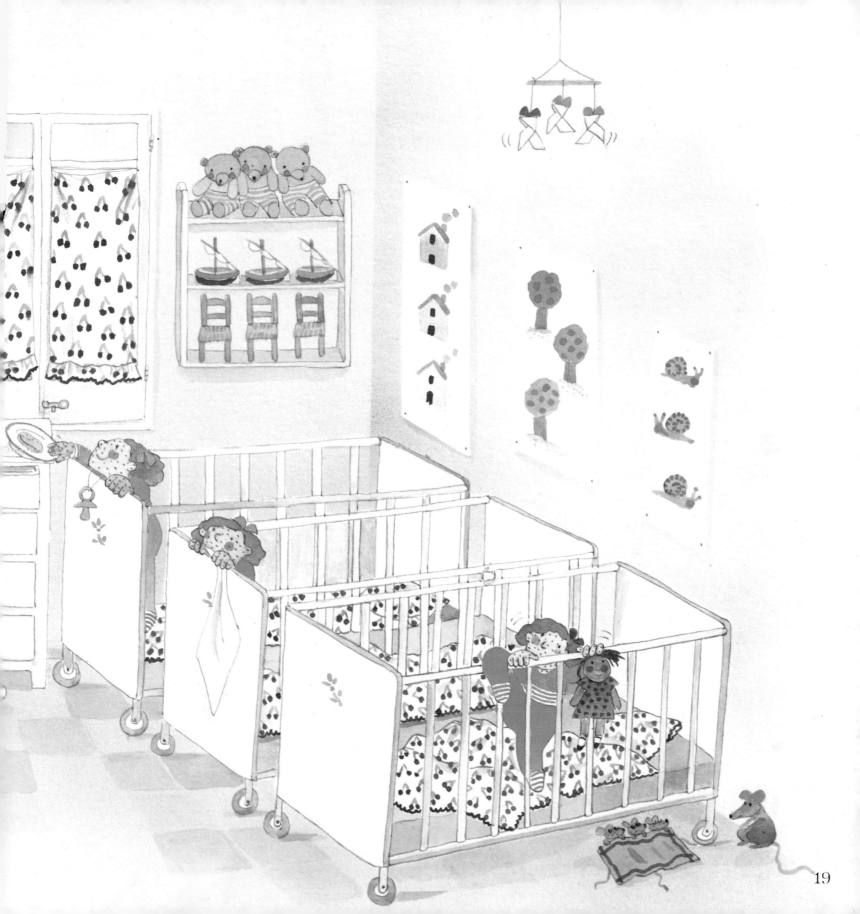

Hello, there! In every picture you'll find lots of things—boys and girls, swings, plates and glasses. But there are other things you'll find—things with pink ears and tiny little tails....Very good! You've guessed it already! In every drawing there are the little mouse Triplets with their mother. If there's anyone who hasn't seen them yet, turn back to the beginning and look for them! Then all of you can make the hanging mobile with the little mice.

Terry